Walt Disney

History Maker Bios

Jane Sutcliffe

LERNER PUBLICATIONS COMPANY • MINNEAPOLIS

For Elise, because it's your turn

llustrations by Tad Butler

Lerner Publications Company
A division of Lerner Publishing Group, Inc.
241 First Avenue North
Minneapolis, MN 55401 U.S.A.

Website address: www.lernerbooks.com

Library of Congress Cataloging-in-Publication Data

Sutcliffe, Jane.
    Walt Disney / by Jane Sutcliffe.
       p.   cm. — (History maker biographies)
    Includes bibliographical references and index.
    ISBN 978-1-58013-704-1 (lib. bdg. : alk. paper)
       1. Disney, Walt, 1901–1966—Juvenile literature. 2. Animators—United States—Biography—Juvenile literature. 3. Motion pictures—Biography—Juvenile literature. I. Disney, Walt, 1901–1966. II. Title.
    NC1766.U52D566 2009
    791.43092—dc22 [B]   2008025152

Manufactured in the United States of America
1 2 3 4 5 6 – PA – 14 13 12 11 10 09

TABLE OF CONTENTS

INTRODUCTION

Walt Disney made the world smile. He created lovable cartoon characters. He made movies with happy endings. He built amusement parks that thrilled millions.

But making people smile was no easy job. It took many hours of hard work. Time after time, Walt failed. He lost money. He lost sleep. But he never lost his determination. And in the end, all those smiles made *Walt Disney* one of the most famous names in the world.

This is his story.

1 A BOY WITH A DREAM

Walt Disney was born on December 5, 1901, in Chicago, Illinois. When he was four years old, the family moved to a farm in Marceline, Missouri. That's where Walt started drawing.

He once drew a picture of his neighbor's horse, Rupert. The neighbor was so pleased he paid Walt a nickel. It was Walt's first sale as an artist. He was about seven years old.

Walt's parents, Elias and Flora, moved the family to Kansas City, Missouri, in 1911. Nine-year-old Walt and his older brother Roy had paper routes. They got up before dawn to deliver papers. After school, they had more papers to deliver.

Somehow Walt still found time to draw. He drew funny pictures at the local barbershop. The barber hung the pictures in the window. People came to the shop even when they didn't need a haircut, just to see Walt's drawings.

Walt (LEFT) stands with Flora (MIDDLE) and his sister, Ruth (RIGHT). Walt also had three older brothers: Herbert, Raymond, and Roy.

Walt decided he wanted to be a professional artist when he grew up. And he seemed to be in a big hurry to grow up.

In 1917, the United States entered World War I (1914–1918). Walt wanted to do his part. So, at sixteen, he lied about his age and joined the Red Cross Ambulance Corps in France. Most of the fighting was taking place in Europe. He didn't see any fighting. Mostly, he ran errands and drove people around. And he drew. He even drew phony war medals on his friends' jackets for fun.

Walt enjoyed his time with the Red Cross. He wrote on this photo: "Doing something I very seldom do — work. Every once in a while I make trips with this truck."

After one year, Walt was back in Kansas City. He heard about a company that was looking for someone to draw ads for the Christmas rush. Walt was hired. The job didn't last long. But for the first time, Walt could call himself a real artist.

Then, in early 1920, he got another job drawing ads. The Kansas City Film Ad Company was starting to make moving cartoon ads to show in movie theaters. There, Walt was not just making drawings. He was making the drawings move! He took photos of drawings that changed slightly from one to the next. When a film ran the photos one after another, the drawings came to life.

Walt was fascinated. He borrowed a book about animated (moving) cartoons from the library and tried to learn all he could. Walt read about new and better ways to make cartoons. He wanted his boss to try out what he'd learned. The boss wasn't interested in Walt's fancy new ideas. He said no. So Walt experimented on his own. He worked in his parents' garage in the evenings.

He came up with his own funny cartoons about things that happened in town. He called them Laugh-O-grams. Walt's Laugh-O-grams were shown in a theater in town. They were a hit.

A LASTING IMPRESSION

Once Walt and his sister found some sticky tar in a barrel. With sticks for paintbrushes, they used the tar to draw pictures on the side of the house. Walt assured Ruth that the tar would wash right off. Of course, it didn't. Those drawings stayed on the house for years.

Then, in 1922, Walt took a very big step.
He started his own company. At twenty
years old, Walt was the head of Laugh-O-
gram Films, Inc. He hired employees. And
he took an even bigger step. He quit his job
at the Film Ad Company.

Walt and his artists started working on
new cartoons. They all had lots of fun.
But the new cartoons didn't make enough
money to pay the artists. The staff soon got
tired of working for no money. One by one,
they left.

Walt's parents had moved away. He had been living in a boardinghouse. He started sleeping in his office to save money. He paid a dime to wash up at a train station.

Soon Walt had fewer and fewer dimes in his pocket. One day, he had none. He wrote to his brother Roy, who was living in California. "You can't do any more than you've done," Roy wrote back. The company was finished.

Walt made movies of babies to get enough money for a train ticket to California. Then he sold his movie camera. In July 1923, he left. He had one suitcase, forty dollars, and one of his films.

And he still had his dream.

2 Making a Mouse Famous

Walt was betting everything on a single film. The little movie was called *Alice's Wonderland*. It was a mix of cartoon characters and a live girl, all playing together. Walt hoped that someone, somewhere, would want to turn his idea into a whole series of *Alices*. No one did.

Walt's Alice was a real girl in a cartoon world.

Then a telegram arrived from New York. A movie distributor there liked the film. She would show it in theaters around the country. She offered Walt a contract for a series of twelve *Alice Comedies*—and maybe more later on.

Walt should have been thrilled. Instead, he was terrified. How could he do this alone? He went to see Roy for advice. Walt showed him the telegram. "What do I do now?" he said. He asked Roy to help him get started. Roy had never made a movie in his life. But he couldn't turn down his brother.

Walt and Roy set up a studio. At first, Walt drew the cartoons. Roy took care of the money and ran the camera. Then they hired employees to help.

Lillian Bounds worked at the studio too. Every night after work, Walt drove Lillian home. He talked and talked about his plans for the studio. Lillian was a good listener. Soon Walt was in love. On July 13, 1925, he and Lillian were married.

Walt (SECOND FROM LEFT) and Lillian (CENTER) were married at Lillian's brother's home in Idaho. The couple pose here with Lillian's family.

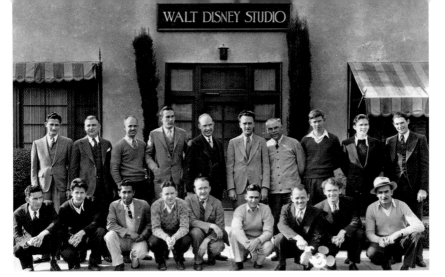

The Disney crew in front of the Walt Disney Studio. Walt is in the bottom row, on the far right.

Things were going well for Walt at last. He moved the studio to a bigger building. A sign over the door announced the "Walt Disney Studio." And when the *Alice Comedies* were done, he came up with a new character. His name was Oswald the Lucky Rabbit. The *Oswald* cartoons were even more popular than the *Alices* had been.

In February 1928, Walt and Lillian took a trip to New York City. Walt was to talk to the distributor about making more Oswald cartoons. (By then, a different distributor had taken over.) But this man had a surprise waiting.

According to the fine print in the contract, he owned the Oswald character. Walt didn't. There was more. The man had gone behind Walt's back. He had hired nearly all Walt's artists away from him. He could make all the Oswald cartoons he wanted. He didn't need Walt.

Walt was stunned. Suddenly he had no staff and no star. He needed a new idea—fast.

Walt's character Oswald the Lucky Rabbit was owned by Charles Mintz. Mintz was the distributor of the Oswald cartoons.

The whole way home on the train, Walt drew. He tried one idea after another. Finally, he settled on a mouse. Proudly, he introduced Lillian to his new cartoon star—Mortimer Mouse.

Mortimer? Lillian thought that was a horrible name for a mouse. Well then, Walt suggested, how about Mickey? And so, Mickey Mouse was born.

Walt's famous creation Mickey Mouse was originally called Mortimer Mouse.

Until then, all Walt's movies—and everyone else's—had no sound. Then some studios began to turn out "talking" films. Walt wanted Mickey to talk and sing too.

But how? No one had yet figured out a way to match up a cartoon's sound and its action. So Walt came up with his own way. He drew a mark on the film every few inches. When the film was played, the marks showed up as flashes on the screen. The flashes marked the beat of music. (Later, a bouncing ball helped to keep the beat.)

IT REALLY HAPPENED!
Walt worked late into the night at the studio. Lillian was often alone. To keep her company, Walt bought her a puppy. He presented it to her in a hatbox on Christmas morning. Years later, he used that scene in his movie *Lady and the Tramp*.

Walt hired musicians to record the music for his cartoon, called *Steamboat Willie*. He added funny noises—whistles and gongs and cowbells. There was even a parrot squawking, "Man overboard!" That voice was Walt's. The sounds helped to tell the story of the cartoon.

On November 18, 1928, *Steamboat Willie* was shown for the first time. Walt was there. He listened as the audience hooted with laughter. His movie was a hit!

Critics went wild over the cartoon too. One reporter said it best: *Steamboat Willie* was "a wow!"

Mickey in STEAMBOAT WILLIE. For years, Walt himself was the voice of Mickey.

3 SNOW WHITE

Mickey Mouse was a movie star. His name was on theater signs. He got fan letters. Soon, cities and towns all over the country had Mickey Mouse Clubs. Children gathered to watch Mickey Mouse cartoons and sing Mickey Mouse songs.

By the 1930s, children were playing with Mickey Mouse toys, eating off Mickey Mouse plates, and telling time with Mickey Mouse watches.

The next year, Walt started a new cartoon series called *Silly Symphonies*. Between those and the Mickeys, his studio would be making as many as thirty-six cartoons in one year. And Walt wanted each one to be better than the last.

The staff worked hard to give Walt what he wanted. But Walt wanted everything to be perfect. That often made him a grumpy boss. He was working too hard and worrying too much. He couldn't sleep. Sometimes he cried. Walt needed a vacation.

In October 1931, Walt and Lillian went on a long trip. When they returned, Walt started exercising. He learned to relax.

But he was still full of new ideas. He wanted his artists to draw characters that looked more real. He wanted arms and legs that looked and moved like real arms and legs. He wanted his characters to act more real too. "I want the characters to be somebody," he liked to say. "I don't want them just to be a drawing." So he hired art teachers to give classes at the studio. The Disney artists spent evenings learning how to make their drawings better than ever.

Walt worked hard to help Disney artists improve their drawing.

Walt had another idea. All of his cartoons so far had been in black and white. Color film was very new. Walt began doing his cartoons in color. His first color cartoon, *Flowers and Trees*, won an Academy Award. And in 1933, *Three Little Pigs* became Walt's most popular cartoon yet.

The Disneys had other reasons to celebrate. In December 1933, Walt and Lillian had a baby daughter. They named her Diane. Several years later, they adopted another daughter, Sharon.

Walt and Lillian with Diane in 1934

SNOW WHITE AND THE SEVEN DWARFS *was the first popular movie-length cartoon.*

All of Walt's big ideas were beginning to pay off. And he was working on an even bigger idea. He would make a full-length cartoon—as long as a regular movie.

Some people said Walt was crazy. The movie would be ten times as long as any of his other cartoons. No one would sit through a jumbo-sized cartoon, they said.

In addition, Walt had chosen the fairy tale "Snow White." It was a rather scary story. Walt had always been known for funny cartoons full of jokes. He was risking his reputation, people said.

Walt didn't listen. He knew exactly the movie he wanted to make. He acted out scenes for his staff. He made faces to demonstrate how this or that character should smile or frown or cry. He knew which kinds of trees or mushrooms should be drawn in the background. It was as if he already saw the whole movie in his head.

In the original fairy tale, the dwarfs were all alike. They didn't even have names. Walt and his staff gave each one his own personality. The Dwarfs were as different as their names: Doc, Happy, Grumpy, Sleepy, Sneezy, Bashful, and Dopey.

HELLO, BURPY

Walt and his staff had to think up all the names for the Dwarfs. Some of the ones they didn't use were Shorty, Tubby, Baldy, Dizzy, and Burpy.

Walt spent three years on *Snow White and the Seven Dwarfs*. As the opening date neared, he and his staff worked morning and night, even on weekends, to finish it. No one complained. They all knew they were creating something wonderful.

In December 1937, *Snow White and the Seven Dwarfs* came to theaters. People lined up for a chance to see the movie. Everywhere, audiences were enchanted by what Walt had created. No one had ever seen anything like it, because nothing like it had ever been made.

Walt had not just created another hit cartoon. He had changed the whole definition of what a cartoon was.

4 WALT DISNEY PRESENTS

*S*now White and the Seven Dwarfs was
a sensation. It broke records for ticket
sales. It won an Academy Award. Best of
all, it made a lot of money for the studio.

Walt knew just what he wanted to do
with that money. He began building a new,
modern studio. Walt fretted over every
detail. He even planned the paint color on
the walls.

Popular child actress Shirley Temple gave Walt his special Academy Award for SNOW WHITE—one big statue and seven dwarf-sized ones.

Before *Snow White* was finished, Walt had been planning other full-length cartoons. In February 1940, *Pinocchio* came to movie theaters. Walt hoped it would be a hit too. It wasn't. Audiences didn't find the same magic and charm in *Pinocchio* that they had seen in *Snow White*. They stayed away.

Walt wanted to try something new. His next idea started as a short Mickey Mouse cartoon. The cartoon would be set to classical music called *The Sorcerer's Apprentice*. Then the idea grew. Other works of music were added. Each had its own cartoon, with everything from dinosaurs to dancing hippos.

Walt called his big idea *Fantasia*. But the movie was too new and different for most people. *Fantasia* was not a hit either.

DEER HERE!

For the movie *Bambi*, Walt wanted the cartoon deer to look as real as live ones. So he brought in live deer for the artists to draw. The deer lived at the studio for over a year. The movie came to theaters in 1942.

Walt's next movie hit, DUMBO, arrived in theaters in 1941.

Instead, it was a little idea that became Disney's next success. *Dumbo* was a sweet story about a baby circus elephant. It was simple and short. And it hadn't cost much to make. But audiences loved it. *Dumbo* was a surprise moneymaker in the fall of 1941.

Then, just weeks later, Japanese planes attacked Pearl Harbor in the Hawaiian Islands. The United States was at war. Suddenly no one was interested in cute little elephants.

Five hundred U.S. soldiers moved into the studio. They were there to protect a nearby airplane factory. They placed guns around the buildings. They stacked bullets in the garages.

Walt discusses a navy training film in 1942.

A navy official asked Walt to make training films for sailors. The films would help the sailors identify enemy planes and ships. And he needed the first one in ninety days! Walt gulped and answered, "Yes, sir!"

Walt made other training films too. Some of them were top secret. By the end of the war in 1945, his studio had turned out miles and miles of film. He hadn't made a profit on any of it.

When the war was over, Walt was bursting with new ideas. He wanted to get right back into making big cartoon movies. His brother Roy was worried about how costly those would be. He wanted to make cheaper movies. Walt wouldn't hear of it. He wouldn't put the Disney name on anything that wasn't the very best.

He dove right in. The first movie, *Cinderella*, was the studio's biggest hit since *Snow White*. *Alice in Wonderland* and *Peter Pan* followed not long after.

Walt (RIGHT) and his brother Roy made a good team. Walt dreamed up movies, and Roy took care of the money.

Walt had always loved animals. He decided to make animals the stars of his next movie. Not cartoon animals—real, live animals in nature.

He sent a husband-and-wife film team to Alaska. He asked them to film the seals there. They spent a whole year. They filmed seals swimming, seals fighting, and seals caring for baby seals. Every so often, they got a message from Walt: "More seals."

Seal Island was released in 1948. Once again, Walt had created something new. He had turned animals into characters people cared about. The next year, *Seal Island* won an Academy Award.

This poster for SEAL ISLAND mentions the movie's Academy Award win.

That same year, Walt flew to Great Britain. He was to oversee the filming of a new movie, *Treasure Island*. The movie was about a boy who joins a band of pirates. It used all real actors—no cartoons. Walt had done live-action filming before. But it had always been mixed in with a cartoon. *Treasure Island* was another first for Walt and the studio.

But that was Walt. He never liked to do the same thing twice. Every big idea had to be bigger than the one before it.

Still, no one dreamed just how big—really big—Walt's next idea would turn out to be.

5 "DISNEYLAND IS YOUR LAND"

Most days—and most nights—Walt was busy at the studio. But he made time for his family too. When his daughters were young, he often took them to an amusement park nearby. He'd sit and watch them ride the carousel for hours.

He noticed other parents doing the same thing. And he wondered, why not build a park where grown-ups can have fun too?

By the early 1950s, "Why not" had turned into "I will." Not only would Walt build a big, grand park. It would be bigger and grander than any park ever built. It would be as magical as his movies. He started calling it Disneyland. The name stuck.

He sent people to inspect amusement parks all over the world. He studied how people moved around the park. He studied the rides. He talked to the owners of the biggest parks in the country. They all said the same thing: what Walt wanted to do couldn't be done. He didn't listen.

Walt points out a drawing of Sleeping Beauty Castle in January 1955.

Walt kept stuffing more and more ideas into his park. The bigger the park grew, the more fun he had. And the more fun he had, the bigger the park grew.

He'd even thought up a way to pay for the park: television. This was a fairly new form of entertainment. But more and more people had TVs in their homes.

Walt agreed to do a weekly TV show for the ABC network. The network would pay Walt money, so he could build the park. And he could tell people watching TV about the park and the Disney movies.

He would call the show—of course—*Disneyland*. (Later the name was changed to *Walt Disney's Wonderful World of Color*.)

Walt (SITTING) signs the contract with ABC for the Disney TV show. Roy is pictured at the far right.

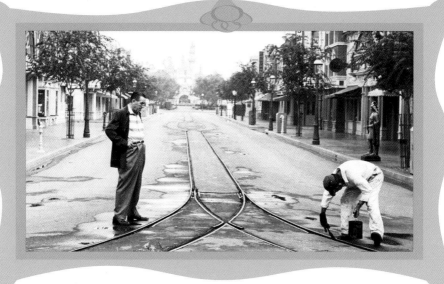

Walt often showed up to see how things were going at his park. He said Disneyland would never be completely finished because he would always be able to add to it.

On July 12, 1954, workers started building Walt's dream park. Walt planned to open the park the next year. He was going to be a very busy man! He often showed up at the work site, just to hurry everyone along.

Just a few months later, his television show was on the air. Walt was the host of the show. At first, he said he was "scared to death" at being on TV. But he never looked nervous. He looked calm and friendly. People started calling him Uncle Walt.

Walt was popular as the host of his TV show.

Many of the episodes showed old Disney cartoons and films. Some were behind-the-scenes stories about new movies like *20,000 Leagues Under the Sea*. In others, Walt talked about Disneyland. He made the park sound like a magical place. And people could watch, little by little, as it was built.

Nobody seemed to mind that Walt's show was mostly a commercial for his park. People loved it. They made the show a hit. And they couldn't wait to see Disneyland for themselves.

On July 17, 1955, Disneyland opened. Thousands came. Cameras were placed around the park to show all the fun on live TV. Walt greeted his guests saying, "To all that come to this happy place: welcome. Disneyland is your land." By the end of that summer, nearly one million people had visited Disneyland.

Walt's park was a success. But he hadn't forgotten about movies. In 1964, the movie *Mary Poppins* combined live action with cartoons. It wowed audiences and won five Academy Awards.

Oops!

Opening day at Disneyland was a mess. It was a blazing hot day. Many of the water fountains didn't work. Neither did some of the rides. Once the sprinklers went off by accident, soaking some of the guests.

In 1964, Walt (CENTER) received the Medal of Freedom from President Lyndon Johnson (RIGHT). That is the highest award given to someone who is not in the military.

By the end of that year, Walt was sixty-three years old. He was one of the most recognized people in the world. He had been awarded the Medal of Freedom by U.S. president Lyndon Johnson. How would he ever top all his big ideas? He decided to try.

He came up with an idea for a new park. This one would be in Florida. Disney World would be more than just a copy of Disneyland. Walt wanted to build a whole new kind of city around his park. It was Walt's grandest idea yet.

He knew an idea this big was going to take years to finish. But, in November 1966, he became sick. Walt had been a smoker for a long time. He had lung cancer. On December 15, 1966, Walt Disney died. He was sixty-five.

Walt had been an artist, an entertainer, and a businessman. But most of all, he'd been a dreamer. He dreamed the impossible and made it possible. Walt Disney showed the world that dreams do come true.

Walt enjoyed children. His films are some of the most popular children's movies ever made.

TIMELINE

In the year . . .

1917   Walt joined the Red Cross Ambulance Corps to serve in World War I.

1920   he got a job with the Kansas City Film Ad Company.

1922   he started Laugh-O-gram Films, Inc.

1923   he moved to California.   `Age 21`

1925   he married Lillian Bounds.

1928   *Steamboat Willie* was first shown in theaters.

1932   his cartoon *Flowers and Trees* won an Academy Award.

1933   his daughter Diane was born.

1936   his daughter Sharon was adopted.

1937   *Snow White and the Seven Dwarfs* was released.   `Age 36`

1941   *Dumbo* was released in October. he began making training films for the U.S. Navy in December.

1949   *Seal Island* won an Academy Award.

1954   his television show began.

1955   Disneyland opened.

1964   he received the Medal of Freedom from President Lyndon Johnson.   `Age 62`

1965   *Mary Poppins* won five Academy Awards.

1966   he died on December 15.   `Age 65`

MAKING THE MAGIC

In Walt's day, nearly all cartoon movies were made the same way. Artists used clear sheets of plastic called cels. The moving parts of a scene were drawn on the cels. Each drawing differed just a bit from the one before it. Each cel was laid over a background drawing. Then it was photographed. When the photos were put together, things appeared to move. A cartoon was born.

Later, things changed. Artists began using computers to create their drawings. Computers allow artists to create cartoons with even more "wows."

Walt might not have recognized a modern cartoon studio. But he would have been thrilled to see how far things have come. He said once, "We keep moving forward—opening new doors and doing new things—because we're curious. And curiosity keeps leading us down new paths."

After all, look where it led Walt.

This cartoon cel from FANTASIA is laid over a background drawing.

FURTHER READING

Conley, Robyn. *Motion Pictures.* **New York: Franklin Watts, 2004.** Learn how live-action movies are made, which inventions make them possible, and how technology continues to change them.

Court, Rob. *How to Draw Cartoons.* **Chanhassen, MN: Child's World, 2005.** This guide gives instructions and tips to help you draw like a real cartoon artist.

Lockman, Darcy. *Computer Animation.* **New York: Benchmark Books, 2001.** Learn more about computer animation and the technology that developed it.

Nardo, Don. *Animation: Drawings Spring to Life.* **San Diego: Lucent Books, 1992.** This book for older readers explains all about how cartoons are made.

Brothers Grimm. *Grimms' Fairy Tales.* **New York : Grosset & Dunlap, 1945.** Several Disney movies have been based on fairy tales from this classic collection.

WEBSITES

The Mouse
http://www.mickey-mouse.com/themouse.htm
A biography of the famous Disney mouse.

Walt Disney: A Biography
http://disney.go.com/vault/read/walt/index.html
Walt's story, for older readers.

Walt Disney Quotes
http://www.justdisney.com/walt_disney/quotes/quotes01
.html
Smart and funny sayings from Walt Disney.

SELECT BIBLIOGRAPHY

Barrier, Michael. *The Animated Man: A Life of Walt Disney.* Berkeley: University of California Press, 2007.

De Roos, Robert. "The Magic Worlds of Walt Disney." *National Geographic*, August 1963.

Gabler, Neal. *Walt Disney: The Triumph of the American Imagination.* New York: Alfred A. Knopf, 2006.

Imagineers. *Walt Disney Imagineering: A Behind-the-Dreams Look at Making the Magic Real.* New York: Hyperion, 1996.

Merritt, Russell, and J. B. Kaufman. *Walt in Wonderland: The Silent Films of Walt Disney.* Baltimore: Johns Hopkins University Press, 1993.

Miller, Diane Disney, and Pete Martin. *The Story of Walt Disney.* New York: Henry Holt and Company, 1956.

INDEX

Acknowledgments

For photographs and artwork: All photos are © Disney Enterprises, Inc.; Courtesy of Everett Collection, pp. 29, 31, 34; © Mark Kauffman/Time & Life Pictures/Getty Images, p. 32; © Hulton Archive/Getty Images, p. 37; Lyndon Baines Johnson Library and Museum, p. 42; Library of Congress (LC-USZC4-13060), p. 45. Front and Back Cover: © Disney Enterprises, Inc.

For quoted material: p. 12, Diane Disney Miller and Pete Martin, *The Story of Walt Disney* (New York: Henry Holt, 1956); p. 14, Michael Barrier, *The Animated Man* (Berkeley: University of California Press, 2007); p. 20, Robert De Roos, "The Magic Worlds of Walt Disney," *National Geographic*, August 1963; p. 23, Russell Merritt and J. B. Kaufman, *Walt in Wonderland: The Silent Films of Walt Disney* (Baltimore: Johns Hopkins University Press, 1993); p. 32, Miller and Martin, *The Story of Walt Disney*; p. 34, Neal Gabler, *Walt Disney: The Triumph of the American Imagination* (New York: Alfred A. Knopf, 2006); p. 39, Barrier, *The Animated Man*; p. 41, JustDisney.com, "Walt Disney Quotes," *JustDisney.com*, 2005, http://www.justdisney.com/walt_disney/quotes/index.html (July 8, 2008); p. 45, Imagineers, *Walt Disney Imagineering: A Behind-the-Dreams Look at Making the Magic Real* (New York: Hyperion, 1996).